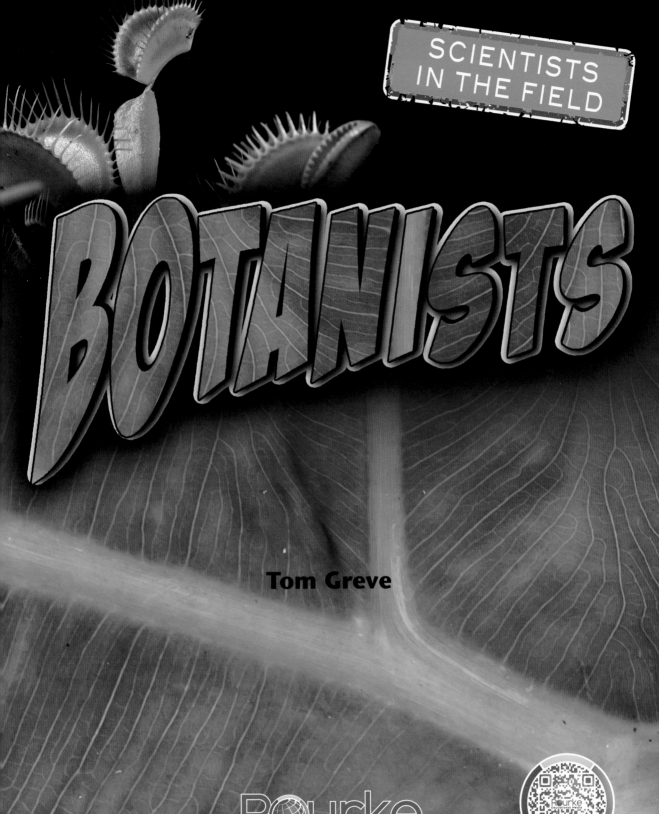

BOTANISTS

Tom Greve

Rourke
Educational Media

rourkeeducationalmedia.com

Scan for Related Titles
and Teacher Resources

Before Reading:

Building Academic Vocabulary and Background Knowledge

Before reading a book, it is important to tap into what your child or students already know about the topic. This will help them develop their vocabulary, increase their reading comprehension, and make connections across the curriculum.

1. *Look at the cover of the book. What will this book be about?*
2. *What do you already know about the topic?*
3. *Let's study the Table of Contents. What will you learn about in the book's chapters?*
4. *What would you like to learn about this topic? Do you think you might learn about it from this book? Why or why not?*
5. *Use a reading journal to write about your knowledge of this topic. Record what you already know about the topic and what you hope to learn about the topic.*
6. *Read the book.*
7. *In your reading journal, record what you learned about the topic and your response to the book.*
8. *After reading the book complete the activities below.*

Content Area Vocabulary
Read the list. What do these words mean?

atmosphere
biology
conservation
deforestation
diversity
ecosystem
extinct
fragrance
genes
genomics
habitat
herbarium
photosynthesis
pollination
reproduce
sustainable

After Reading:

Comprehension and Extension Activity

After reading the book, work on the following questions with your child or students in order to check their level of reading comprehension and content mastery.

1. *Why is it important that botanists work with other scientists such as ecologists? (Summarize)*
2. *What could happen if plants were destroyed? (Infer)*
3. *In what ways are you similar to a plant? (Text to self connection)*
4. *How is the study of plants connected to the study of diseases? (Summarize)*
5. *What role do plants have in ecosystems? (Asking questions)*

Extension Activity

Using what you learned in the text, create a diagram that explains plant pollination. Be sure to label and explain each step. Present your diagram to your teacher, classmates, or parents. Do they understand pollination?

TABLE OF CONTENTS

IT'S ALIVE!

The Sun sets over a lonely desert. Near the bottom of a rocky ridge, a scientist sits near a small group of wildflowers. As pretty as the flowers are, the scientist is not there simply to admire their yellow petals. She is a botanist at work in the field, trying to understand some of the longest-running mysteries of life on planet Earth.

FIELD NOTES

A botanist is a scientist who studies plants. Like doctors who specialize in a wide range of medical studies, botanists can be experts in many different matters of plant life.

It is easy to know that people are alive. They can move, speak, and do all sorts of things that show they are living, breathing, and thinking. The same is true for animals. But what about plants?

Sometimes the easiest way to know a plant is living is to notice its growth. Some plants grow slowly. Others can grow quickly enough to see changes almost every day.

Bamboo trees are among the fastest-growing plants on Earth. In the right conditions, some bamboo trees can grow as much as 35 inches (.89 meters) in a single day!

The Saguaro cactus grows very slowly. In its first 10 years of life, a single cactus will grow to be less than two inches (five centimeters) high. But they can live to be 200 years old, and eventually reach 40 to 60 feet (12-18 meters) in height.

Plants, trees, grass, or anything that grows from soil are just as alive as people and animals. In some ways, plants live very differently than us. In other ways, they live as we do. Plants need food, they work to **reproduce**, and they can adapt to conditions around them.

BREAKTHROUGH BOTANIST

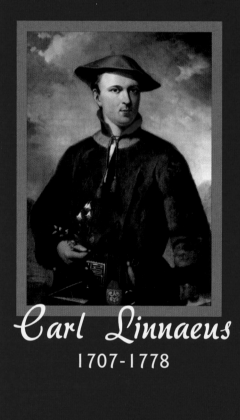

Carl Linnaeus
1707-1778

Though humans have harvested, eaten, and even used plants as medicine throughout history, the science of botany has blossomed in recent centuries. In the 1700s, Swedish scientist Carl Linnaeus helped make sense of the **diversity** of Earth's plants and animals by classifying all living things based on physical characteristics. As a botanist, he classified plants based partly on how they reproduced. Linnaeus's ideas and research became central to botanical understanding long after he died. His work remains important to this day.

Scientists use the Greek words Plantae and Animalia to classify things as plants or animals. The Kingdom of Plantae includes all known species of plants, just as the Kingdom of Animalia includes all known species of animals—including human beings.

KINGDOM PLANTAE

Mosses

Liverworts

Ferns

Club Moss

Cone-Bearing Plants

Flowering Plants

Botanists study the life and **biology** of plants. Their work plays an important role in understanding the complex relationships among Earth's plants, as well as the relationship between plants, animals, and people.

Breakthroughs in plant understanding, whether from the tiny Wolffia plant, or the giant Sequoia tree, happen because of previous scientific research. We know things about the nature of plants that previous generations could not have imagined. This is true thanks in large part to the efforts of botanists.

Watermeal plants, also called duckweed, are the smallest flowering plants on Earth. Each tiny speck is an individual plant.

California's giant sequoia trees are the largest on Earth. They are a coniferous plant, meaning they produce pine cones. They can grow to be 280 feet (85.3 meters) high. That's as tall as a 25-story building. The trees can live to be more than 3,000 years old.

SIPS AND THE SUN

   Botanists have identified the single most important skill of plants on Earth: plants can create food and energy from little more than sunlight, water, and a naturally occurring chemical reaction called **photosynthesis**.

   The Sun, despite being a boiling cauldron of burning gas, is responsible for keeping plants, animals, and people alive. Botanists have found that plants are among Earth's most important resources in keeping the Sun's furious heat at bay.

THE SUN IS HOT, BUT PLANTS ARE COOL

   When the summer sun gets uncomfortably hot, plants release water vapor into the air from their leaves. This action cools the plants down and the vapor cools the surrounding air. The highest leaves in the treetops of a forest—known as the canopy—can release enough water vapor to form clouds that block the hot Sun. The water vapor eventually returns to the plants in the form of rain.

and animals use oxygen to breathe and stay alive. The
ere protecting Earth from the Sun's harmful effects also
en. Thanks to the process of photosynthesis, plants are
y creating more oxygen to keep the planet supplied.

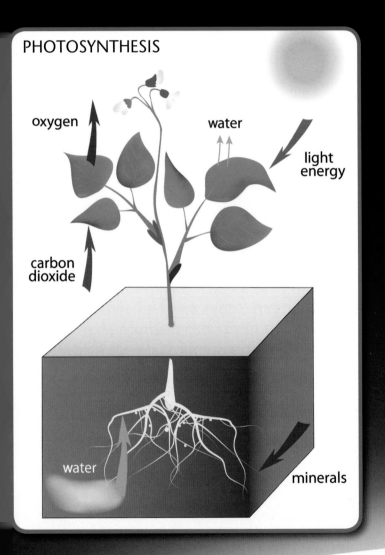

PHOTOSYNTHESIS

oxygen

water

light
energy

carbon
dioxide

water

minerals

SUN AND RAIN SUSTAIN

If a person is hungry, they can go to the kitchen and find something to eat. Plants however, feed themselves without eating. Through photosynthesis, plants convert water and light into sugar, which they store as food. At the same time, they turn carbon dioxide into breathable oxygen. This makes plant life perfectly efficient. They create something beneficial to all life by using **sustainable** light from the Sun and rainwater.

Earth's atmosphere is a protective layer of gas surrounding the entire planet like a blanket. The blanket relies on oxygen released by plants in order to remain healthy and effective. Despite the distance plants on the ground pass benefits all the way to the edge of space.

POKING AROUND OUR PLANET OF PLANTS

Like most scientists, botanists work in both the laboratory as well as the field. After all, the only way to study plants in their natural **habitat** is be outdoors with the plants. Though plants are just as alive as people, they are in many ways more diverse. Because of this, botany is like a big science umbrella, with many areas of plant study underneath it. Each type of study increases botanical understanding for the benefit of all life on Earth.

BOTANY: SCIENTIFIC STUDY OF PLANTS

These are just four of the many types of scientific expertise at work within the overall study of botany.

Agronomists

Plants are Earth's greatest food source. Understanding the best ways and conditions to increase and maintain crop health helps feed the world.

Chemists

Plants are like chemical factories. Understanding plant chemistry has led to countless advances in medicine.

Botany is a life science. Other kinds of sciences include physical sciences such as chemistry, and Earth sciences such as geology.

Ecologists

Plants provide for and receive benefts from other living things in their habitat. Understanding this interconnected relationship between plants, animals, people, and the environment has benefited not just humans, but the entire planet.

Horticulturists

Plants, whether ornamental or edible, are beautiful. Practicing the best ways to promote plant health and diversity within a single garden or locale is a scientific art form that makes Earth a prettier and sustainable planet.

Plants keep us breathing, and they help feed the world. They also hold secrets about reproduction and survival. Plants play the central role in sustaining the overall health of what scientists call an **ecosystem**.

Scientists who study the interaction of plants with other living things in an ecosystem are ecologists.

An ecosystem can be as large as an ocean, or as small as a tree stump. It includes all living things within a specific space.

BREAKTHROUGH BOTANIST

Perhaps no person was more instrumental in developing the modern understanding of botany and ecosystems than Henry Chandler Cowles. By doing field research on certain plants growing in sand dunes along the Great Lakes, he found some species of plants adapted to changes in their environment while others died off. He worked to prove that plants, animals, and even the soil within a single ecosystem depend on each other for survival. He later helped form the **conservation** movement, to preserve wilderness areas and natural habitats.

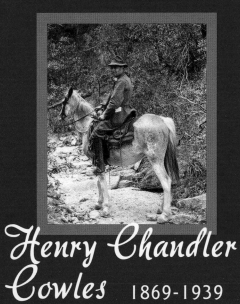

Henry Chandler Cowles 1869-1939

CANADA

Great Lakes

UNITED STATES

Botanists constantly work to learn more about plants and ecosystems by conducting field research. These projects require scientists to spend great amounts of time observing and documenting plant behaviors in specific places, conditions, and times. Some field research is purely for scientific reasons, while other research might be for commercial or business interests.

FIELD NOTES

NSF

Money for many botanical field research projects comes from the federal government's National Science Foundation. The United States Congress created the NSF in part to promote the progress of science. Universities and corporations also fund some research projects. Sometimes scientists pay for their own projects.

Trees are just giant plants. Industries such as timber processing rely on botanical research to understand the best ways to harvest trees without harming the overall forest ecosystem so the trees will grow back. This is one form of conservation, which sustains the supply of a specific natural resource.

BOTANICAL BATTLEFIELD

BUSINESS vs ECOSYSTEMS

In the face of large profits, sometimes conservation loses. **Deforestation**, or the harvesting of an entire forest in order to sell the land for a different use, permanently damages the entire ecosystem, from the soil to the animals, and even the people. Deforestation is an example of habitat destruction.

The reasons for botany field research can be as varied as the plants botanists might be studying. One project might study possible reasons for the spread of a disease in a specific species of tree. Another might be to determine the effects of forest fires on certain plants and their reproduction in a mountain range. Sometimes researchers even set out to discover new species of plants.

Like people, plants can suffer from diseases and viruses. Apiognomonia veneta is a pathogen that affects trees. Botanists can often diagnose and treat plant illnesses.

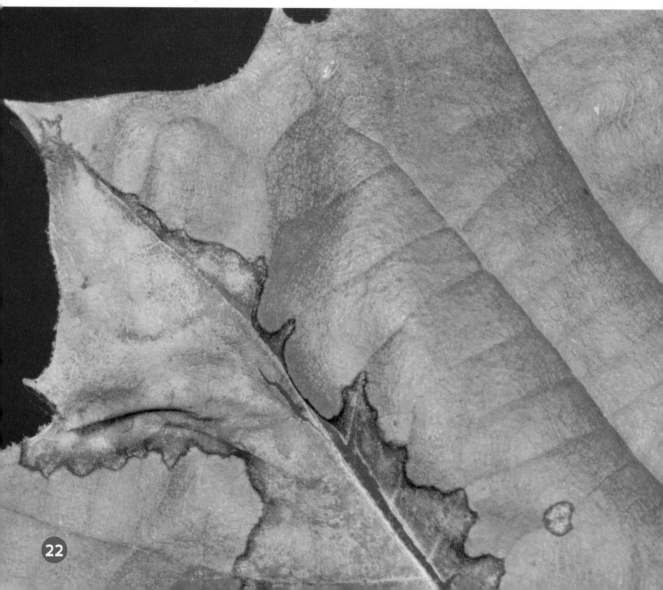

THE REPRODUCTIVE CYCLE

Any living thing has to reproduce or it will eventually become **extinct**. Human reproduction requires a male and a female to connect physically. Plant reproduction is more complex and varied.

There are male plants and female plants, and some plants that are both at the same time. Some plants can reproduce by themselves.

Botany's Miracle of Life

Flowering plants offer a glimpse into the fragile and fascinating world of plant reproduction and the reasons healthy ecosystems allow the process to sustain itself.

Flowering plants reproduce through **pollination**. This means pollen from a male plant fertilizes the egg of a female plant. The movement of the pollen happens thanks to pollinators such as bees, moths, and even some small birds that find the bright flowers and the nectar inside irresistible. They land on a flower and pollen sticks to their bodies. When they fly away and land on another flower, the pollen rubs off on the flower's female parts and creates a seed. That seed becomes a baby plant that will take root and grow.

Birds and bees are common pollinators. That means they cause plants to reproduce. If someone uses the phrase "the birds and the bees," it means they are talking about reproduction, though birds and bees help in the reproduction of flowering plants, not people or animals.

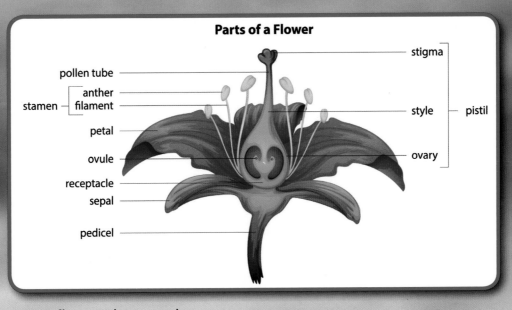

Parts of a Flower

- stigma
- pollen tube
- anther
- filament
- stamen
- petal
- ovule
- receptacle
- sepal
- pedicel
- style
- ovary
- pistil

Most flowers have male reproductive parts and female reproductive parts. They produce pollen through the stamen or male parts. They can also receive pollen from a bird, bee, or other pollinator through their pistils, which include the stigma, style, and ovary. Flowers are colorful because it helps attract pollinators.

This reproductive dance works for the plants as long as there is a healthy population of pollinators like birds and bees to do the job. Lately scientists have noticed there are fewer and fewer bees. Massive scientific efforts are underway to find out why.

The decline of pollinators threatens the reproduction of much of the world's plants and, as a result, the world's food supply.

↓

The decline of the plants means less oxygen due to diminished photosynthesis.

↓

Less oxygen affects all life on Earth. This is why the work of botanists connects in countless ways to the work of ecologists, horticulturists, and other scientists. Research and understanding from one field helps the others.

Honeybees are great pollinators. But a growing amount of research shows they are declining in number, in part because of widespread use of chemical pesticides on farmlands.

BREAKTHROUGH BOTANIST

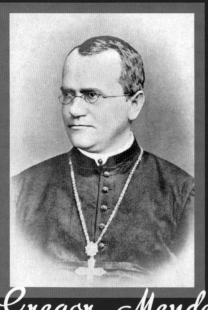

Gregor Mendel

1822-1884

One botanist who made important discoveries about plant reproduction was Gregor Mendel. But, in fact, he wasn't really a botanist at all! He was a priest who loved gardening and science. By studying pea plants, he found that plants, like humans, inherit physical traits from their ancestors. His discovery altered the path of modern botany and medicine. Now we call those inherited traits **genes**. Genetics, or the study of genes, is at the forefront of medical research.

It is a fast-growing and important science because it can unlock mysteries of why certain diseases affect some people, but not others. It all started with Gregor Mendel's peas.

Mendel used pea plants because they are easy to grow and their reproduction is easily controlled. They have male and female parts so Mendel could let some of his peas self-pollinate or he could cross-pollinate others by hand.

Researching Remote Reproduction

Right now, field research botanists are working in the New Mexico desert to study evening primrose plants. The flowers from these plants give off a scent that attracts moths for pollination, but also attracts caterpillars, which eat the plants. Botanists want to know if some of these plants are reducing their smell to improve their chances of reproducing in desert locations where plants are longer distances from one another. The project uses botany, ecology, and the promise of genetics to study a mystery of life flowering high on the desert plain.

evening primrose

The Sphinx moth, also called a hawk moth, has a long tongue specifically used to pollinate flowers. Moths mostly fly in the evening or after dark, unlike butterflies, which fly around in broad daylight.

The botanists working on the evening primrose research project spend days at a time in the desert looking for the plants and the pollinating moths. Once located, they measure flower sizes and shapes, collect samples of flowers and pollen from the moths, and even capture the actual flower scent by pumping its **fragrance** into tiny bottles. They record the data, mark the exact locations of the plants using a global positioning satellite (GPS) device, and finally, once they complete their documentation, they put their samples in a **herbarium** for further genetic study into the plant's behavior.

Herbariums are storage holders for plants taken from the field during research. Depending on the plant in question, specimens are mounted on paper and pressed with a light wood frame quickly, so they don't deteriorate.

Doing field research requires heavy duty planning ahead of time. Researchers must find locations where certain plants exist and determine every piece of scientific equipment they'll need with them at the site, no matter how remote.

The research into the pollination practices of evening primrose plants, along with countless other botany field research projects, is increasingly moving into the science of **genomics**.

Genomics, or the study of the complete set of genes in any living thing, allows botanists to know far more about plant biology than ever before. Genomic studies likely represent the next wave of great biological discoveries about plants and people too.

DNA

Plants, like humans and animals, are made up of cells. Deep within these cells are strands of DNA, which are like genetic building blocks. But plant DNA has one big difference from human or animal DNA. Plant cells have chloroplasts, which are the secret behind a plant's ability to perform photosynthesis.

BREAKTHROUGH BOTANIST

Barbara McClintock

1902-1992

Barbara McClintock is one of the great figures of the modern era of botanical and genomic research. Her study of corn plants led to her discovery of genetic mutations, or jumping genes. This showed how corn can change color over generations, and led to a new understanding of how diseases change over time and why human genetics change as well. In 1983, she became the first female to win an unassisted Nobel Prize for medicine.

BACKYARD BOTANISTS

The world is full of amateur botanists, researchers, and people who are simply enthusiastic about plants. Nowhere can these people enjoy their passion more, both in practice and research, than in a garden. Gardens are like botanical research projects themselves!

For many botanists, their lifelong passion for plants and the natural world began in a garden. If you love being outside, surrounded by natural beauty, you might become a botanist.

A master gardener creates beauty and ecological diversity based on their knowledge of many things, including botany. It is a science and an art form.

There is no better way to get up close with the wonders of plant life and the beauty of botany than to dig in with both hands.

The best part about planting and maintaining a garden is that anyone with an interest in plants, science, or in simply watching life unfold in their backyard can do it.

Master gardeners often keep journals to note their successes, failures, and specific observations about plants.

Species: Caryopteris Clandonesis or Blue Mist Shrub

Woody shrubs growing near the door. Lovely flowers in fall. Transplants easily with long root systems and recovers in one moist, shady day. Stems break easily at the base. Pollen gatherers love them in late summer.

Many of the most advanced botanists found their passion for plants and nature by spending time outdoors as youngsters.

If plant life and the natural world of botanical studies interest you, getting involved can be as simple as taking some seeds from vegetables in the kitchen. Just plant them in soil in a sunny spot where they can easily be watered by the rain or by hand and let nature take over. Soon you'll have your own botanical research project come to life.

Some fruit or vegetable seeds can be planted directly into outdoor soil. Others need to first be planted in pots or small containers and transplanted into the garden after they sprout. Regardless, it's important to make sure the seeds are from a healthy, ripe fruit or vegetable to give them the best chance to grow.

"Attention young botanists! Pay attention to the world around you. Take walks through your neighborhood, in the woods, a meadow, or near a pond. Get a plant field guide. Go to public gardens. Look and listen, and nature will speak to you."

-Deb Quantock McCarey,
Plant Enthusiast, Botanical Journalist, Gardening Blogger

BEGINNING BACKYARD BOTANY IN BRIEF

Plant some seeds and watch them grow
With soil, water, and sunlight, soon you will know

Something special Earth offers for free,
To all things planted, growing healthy and green

There's life in the Sun, there's life in the ground,
Add water and wait ... living plants will abound

Plants and flowers cover the Earth,
It's hard to calculate what they are worth

Without these plants, we couldn't survive,
They produce oxygen, to help us all thrive

They keep the bees buzzing and the birds busy too
Without them, healthy habitats would be few

Besides all that, a garden's true highlight,
Is color and fragrance, a sensory delight

Botanists keep researching to understand more,
About keeping plants alive and well, forevermore

Another good way a young person can explore an interest in botany is to get involved in citizen-scientist ventures with a local university or botanical organization.

Research projects often use citizen-scientist helpers. Volunteers may work on documenting how many individual plants of a certain kind are alive within a specific habitat. This is a great way for interested young people to get firsthand experience with research in the field.

Citizen scientists in and around San Francisco are systematically monitoring several plant species unique to the habitat around the San Francisco Bay. They note the thriving species and those becoming less common in response to changes, such as new road and home construction.

WAYS TO GET INVOLVED

There are easy outlets for students to explore their interest in plant science beyond the classroom. Museums, botanical gardens, and even gardening clubs offer youngsters the chance to work on real research projects.

Even in areas like Chicago, a huge city where plant life might seem limited, citizen-scientist opportunities abound. *Inquiry Adventures*—through the University of Illinois—lets students collect observations, measure, and document botanical events in some of the city's forest preserves.

Botanical gardens were first designed to cultivate and study plants for their medicinal or healing properties. Over time, these gardens have become centers of understanding not only for a wide range of plant species, but also the effects that changes in the environment have on them. Botanical gardens give visitors a chance to gain deeper knowledge about the curious nature of plants.

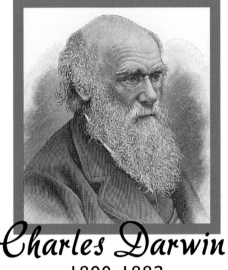

Charles Darwin
1809-1882

George W. Carver
1860-1943

TIMELINE

300 BCE
Ancient Greeks celebrate, study plants formally.

1500
German scientists document medicinal uses for various plants.

1600s
English scientists begin using microscope to detect cells in plants.

1700s
Carl Linnaeus classifies known plants by appearance, behavior.

1800s
Naturalist Charles Darwin produces natural selection theory.

1800s
Gregor Mendel discovers trait inheritance in peas.

1900s
George W. Carver popularizes crop rotation.

1900s
H.C. Cowles's field research becomes basis for study of ecology.

1983
Barbara McClintock wins Nobel Prize for corn genetics studies.

2000
George Stebbins, plant and genetic evolution theorist, dies at age 94.

Glossary

atmosphere (AT-muhss-fihr): protective layer of gas surrounding Earth

biology (bye-OL-uh-jee): scientific study of living things

conservation (kon-sur-VAY-shuhn): protection of natural resources

deforestation (de-for-eh-STAY-shuhn): cut down forests without replanting

diversity (di-VUR-suh-tee): variety

ecosystem (EK-oh-sis-tuhm): group of animals and plants related to their environment

extinct (eg-STINKT): no longer alive on Earth

fragrance (FRAY-gruhnss): odor produced by plants, flowers

genes (JEENZ): inherited cells of all living things

genomics (jeh-NO-miks): the study of all inherited cells in all living things

habitat (HAB-uh-tat): place and natural conditions a plant or animal lives in

herbarium (ur-BAR-ee-uhm): a container for plant specimens

photosynthesis (foh-toh-SIN-thuh-siss): chemical process used by plants to make food and oxygen

pollination (pahl-eh-NAY-shuhn): the process by which flowers reproduce

reproduce (re-pro-DOOS): create offspring

sustainable (Seh-STAIN-uh-buhl): a process that keeps going without help

Index

Show What You Know

1. What is the name of the process that plants use to feed themselves?
2. Which botanist's discovery led to the study of genetics?
3. What is one way for flowering plants to reproduce?
4. What are some other scientific disciplines within the study of botany?
5. What is an easy way for a person to begin learning about botany?

Websites to Visit

www.chicagobotanic.org

www.botany.org

www.kidsgardening.org

About the Author

Tom Greve lives in Chicago with his wife and two kids. An occasional gardener, he is intrigued by the work of research scientists and the effects their work can have on everyday life for all living things.

Meet The Author!
www.meetREMauthors.com

www.rourkeeducationalmedia.com

PHOTO CREDITS: Cover: botanists © chinaface, venus flytrap © David Huntley Creative, leaf background © ratchanon klamtawee; field notes paper throughout © Anan Kaewkhammul; page 4-5 © IrinaK, inset photo page 4 © Leah-Anne Thompson; page 6-7 © Pieter De Pauw, inset photo © onside; page 9 moss © artincamera, fern © Light & Magic Photography, club moss © Audrey M Vasey, cone © Peter Turner Photography, flowers © Jon Bilous; page 10 © Christian Fischer, page 11 © Yongyut Kumsri; page 12-13 © Stephane Bidouze; page 14-15 © Johan Swanepoel, photosynthesis illustration © Designua; page 16 © left © Budimir Jevtic, right © Leah-Anne Thompson, page 17 left © National Park Service, Alaska Region, right © stefanolunardi; page 18 top © Goodluz, bottom © Nicolas Primola, page 19 courtesy of Yale University Manuscripts & Archives Digital Images Database, map © AridOcean; page 20 courtesy of Gary Peeples/USFWS www.fws.gov/asheville, page 21top left © Oregon_BLM_Forestry_06, top right © Joseph Sohm; page 21 bottom © Joseph Sohm; page 22 © Clemson University - USDA Cooperative Extension Slide Series, Bugwood.org; page 23 © atm2003, page 23 bottom © ksana2010; page 24-25 © chunking, flower illustration © BlueRingMedia, bee illustration © eva_mask; page 26-27 © Leonid Ikan; page 28 peas © ksana2010, page 29 © Stan Shebs; page 30 © Ian Maton, page 31 top © rudigobbo, bottom © National Park Service, Alaska Region; page 32 © Sur, page 33 corn © design56; page 34-35 © kavram; page 36 © Goodluz, page 37 © Dan Kosmayer; page 38 ©Christian Jung, page 39 © FamVeld; page 40 and 41 © Photodiem; page 42-43 © Gina Smith; page 44 © elesi

Edited by: Keli Sipperley

Cover and Interior design by: Nicola Stratford   www.nicolastratford.com

Library of Congress PCN Data

Botanists / Tom Greve
(Scientists in the Field)
ISBN 978-1-63430-412-2 (hard cover)
ISBN 978-1-63430-512-9 (soft cover)
ISBN 978-1-63430-604-1 (e-Book)
Library of Congress Control Number: 2015931713

Also Available as:

Printed in the United States of America, North Mankato, Minnesota